WORLD CUP FEVER

WORLD CUP 2014

AN UNAUTHORIZED GUIDE

Michael Hurley

Raintree
Chicago, Illinois

© 2014 Raintree
an imprint of Capstone Global Library, LLC
Chicago, Illinois

To contact Capstone Global Library please phone 800-747-4992, or visit our website www.capstonepub.com

All rights reserved. No part of this publication may be reproduced or transmitted in any form or by any means, electronic or mechanical, including photocopying, recording, taping, or any information storage and retrieval system, without permission in writing from the publisher.

Edited by Claire Throp and Vaarunika Dharmapala
Designed by Joanna Hinton-Malivoire
Picture research by Hannah Taylor
Originated by Capstone Global Library Limited
Printed and bound in the United States of America, North Mankato, Minnesota.

18 17 16 15 14
10 9 8 7 6 5 4 3 2 1

Library of Congress Cataloging-in-Publication Data
Hurley, Michael, 1979-
 World Cup 2014 / Michael Hurley.
  p. cm.—(World cup fever)
 Includes bibliographical references and index.
 ISBN 978-1-4109-5518-0 (pb)
 1. World Cup (Soccer)—Juvenile literature. I. Title.

GV943.49.H88 2014
796.334668—dc23   2012042866

Acknowledgments
We would like to thank the following for permission to reproduce photographs: Corbis pp. 23 (EPA/Kerim Okten); Getty Images pp. 7 (Gabriel Rossi/LatinContent), 8 (Steve Allen), 9 (Andre Vieira/MCT), 11 (Simon Maina/AFP), 12 (Emiliano Lasalvia/LatinContent), 19 (Cameron Spencer), 20 (Laurence Griffiths), 21 (Alex Livesey), 22 (AFP Photo/Andrew Yates), 25 (Vista Previa/LatinContent), 28 (AFP Photo/Javier Soriano), 33 (Nuno Guimaraes/LatinContent), 35 (Clive Rose), 36 (AFP/Heuler Andrey), 37 (Dean Mouhtaropoulos); Photoshot pp. 5 (Picture Alliance), 13 & 17 (Kyodo), 14 (Actionplus), 15 (Xinhua), 18 (Imago), 26 (ActionPlus); Press Association pp. 10 (AP), 24 (Demotix), 27 (DPA), 29 (Empics), 30 (PA Archive), 31 (Turkpix); SuperStock p. 39 (Age Fotostock).

All background images courtesy of Shutterstock.

Cover photograph of Carles Puyol and Iker Casillas celebrating Spain's win at the 2010 World Cup, reproduced with permission of Getty Images (FIFA/ Mike Hewitt).

Every effort has been made to contact copyright holders of any material reproduced in this book. Any omissions will be rectified in subsequent printings if notice is given to the publisher.

All the Internet addresses (URLs) given in this book were valid at the time of going to press. However, due to the dynamic nature of the Internet, some addresses may have changed, or sites may have changed or ceased to exist since publication. While the author and publisher regret any inconvenience this may cause readers, no responsibility for any such changes can be accepted by either the author or the publisher.

006888CG14

CONTENTS

THE WORLD CUP 4
WORLD CUP 2014 6
BRAZIL: THE HOST NATION 8
TEAMS TO WATCH 12
PLAYERS TO WATCH 18
WORLD CUP FIRST TIMERS 24
MANAGER PROFILES 28
CITIES AND STADIUMS 32
WORLD CUP 2014: THE TEAMS 40
WORLD CUP 2014: MATCH SCHEDULE . 42
GLOSSARY 44
FIND OUT MORE 46
INDEX 48

THE WORLD CUP

The FIFA World Cup is an international soccer tournament that takes place every four years.

The World Cup is played in the summer when, for most of the world's soccer playing nations, there is a break in the league schedule. This allows all of the top players to be available to represent their countries at the World Cup.

The first World Cup was played in Uruguay in South America, in 1930. The popularity of soccer was increasing after two successful Olympic soccer tournaments in 1924 and 1928. Uruguay had won both of the Olympic titles and was chosen to host the first World Cup.

Thirteen soccer teams representing countries from all over the world were invited to take part. More than half of the teams were from South America. Not many teams from Europe played in the inaugural World Cup because it was such a long way to travel, and the trip by boat took weeks. Uruguay beat Argentina 4–2 in the first ever World Cup final.

DID YOU KNOW?

A gold star on a team shirt at the World Cup signifies that the country has won it before. Brazil has five stars on their team shirts as they have won the competition five times. Countries who are permitted to wear stars are:

Brazil (5)
Italy (4)
Germany (3)
Argentina (2)
Uruguay (4)
England (1)
France (1)
Spain (1)

THE 2010 WORLD CUP

The 2010 World Cup was held in South Africa. Spain won the World Cup for the first time in their history. They beat the Netherlands 1–0 in the final after extra time.

2010 WORLD CUP FINAL MATCH REPORT

Date: Friday, July 11, 2010

Venue: Soccer City Stadium, Johannesburg, South Africa

Referee: Howard Webb (England)

Winner: Spain (1–0 against the Netherlands)

Winning goal: Andrés Iniesta, 116th minute

WORLD CUP 2014

The 2014 FIFA World Cup will be held in Brazil. Teams from 32 countries around the world will take part.

The host nation for the World Cup does not have to qualify to play in the competition. The other teams—all 209 of them—have to play a series of matches against teams from the same continent in order to qualify for the World Cup. Qualifying for the World Cup is a long process, and some teams can play as many as 24 matches! The prestige and honor of playing at the World Cup is the reward for getting through the qualifying rounds.

DID YOU KNOW?

Fuleco is the official mascot of the 2014 World Cup in Brazil. He is based on an endangered species of armadillo that can be found in Brazil. The *Tolypeutes tricinctus*, or "tata-bola" in Portuguese, that Fuleco is based on can roll into a ball to protect itself.

THE FINALS

The tournament itself kicks off on June 12, 2014 in the city of São Paulo in Brazil, and the final will be played on Sunday July 13 in Rio de Janeiro. The 32 teams will be placed into eight groups of four. Each team will play three group matches, gaining three points for a win, one point for a draw, and no points for losing. The two teams from each group with the most points will go through to the second round. The tournament then becomes a knockout competition.

▼ **Uruguay's Diego Forlan loses out to Argentina's Ángel di María in a qualifying match for the 2014 World Cup.**

BRAZIL: THE HOST NATION

Brazil was chosen by FIFA to host the 2014 World Cup. It will be the 20th edition of the competition, and it is the second time that Brazil has been the host country.

DID YOU KNOW?

In the 1950s a new city was created in Brazil. The city was called Brasilia, and it replaced Rio de Janeiro as the capital city of Brazil.

Brazil is the fifth largest country in the world and has a population of 199 million people. Brazil is the largest country in South America and its two largest cities are São Paulo and Rio de Janeiro. Rio de Janeiro was chosen by the International Olympics Committee (IOC) to be the host city for the 2016 Olympics.

BRAZIL, A VERY BRIEF HISTORY...

The Portuguese explorer Pedro Álvares Cabral reached Brazil in 1500. Portugal colonized Brazil in the early 1530s and controlled the country until 1822, when Brazil declared independence. In 1889 Brazil became a republic, with a president as the head of state. A military dictatorship controlled the country between 1964 and 1985. In 2011 Dilma Rousseff was democratically elected as president of Brazil. She is the first female president in the country's history.

BRAZIL AND SOCCER

Soccer is the most popular sport in Brazil. There are almost 30,000 soccer teams and more than two million officially registered players. Brazil has a proud history at the World Cup having won the tournament five times.

DID YOU KNOW?

Over a third of all the coffee in the world comes from Brazil.

FAMOUS SOCCER STAR

Brazil has had many great soccer players, but the best known is Pelé (see above, left). Pelé is perhaps the greatest and most famous player of all time. He played for Brazil between 1957 and 1971, and made 91 appearances before retiring from international soccer.

Pelé played at four World Cup tournaments and was part of a successful Brazil team on three occasions, when the team won the trophy in 1958, 1962, and 1970. Pelé had an incredible goal scoring record at the World Cup, with 12 goals in 14 matches.

DID YOU KNOW?

Many Brazilian players have nicknames. Pelé's real name is Edson Arantes do Nascimento. Another famous Brazil player with a nickname is Ronaldinho. His full name is Ronaldo de Assis Moreira.

FAMOUS BRAZILIANS

Felipe Massa (born 1981)

Felipe Massa is another Brazilian sportsman who is recognized all over the world. Massa is a Formula 1 driver, which means he is at the highest level of motor racing. In 2006 Massa started racing for the world-famous Ferrari team, and he has won 11 Grand Prix races for them. In 2008 Felipe Massa was the runner-up in the Formula 1 World Championship.

Oscar Niemeyer (1907 to 2012)

Oscar Niemeyer was an architect, and was responsible for many of the buildings in the new capital, Brasilia. His designs include the President's Palace and the Ministry of Justice. The iconic United Nations (UN) building in New York was also based on Niemeyer's design.

Gisele Bündchen (born 1980)

Gisele Bündchen is a Brazilian model and actress. She is also a UN Goodwill Ambassador. Gisele is married to Tom Brady, an American NFL quarterback. Together, they are one of the most famous couples in the world.

TEAMS TO WATCH

Here are some of the teams that are expected to be successful, or that could cause shock results, at the 2014 World Cup in Brazil.

UNDER PRESSURE

Brazil has played at every World Cup and is the most successful team in the tournament's history. As hosts for the 2014 World Cup, there will be huge expectation from the fans for Brazil to succeed on home soil. Brazil has a vibrant young team, full of skillful players.

TEAM PROFILE

Brazil

World Cup appearances: 19
World Cup wins: 5
2010 World Cup result: quarterfinal

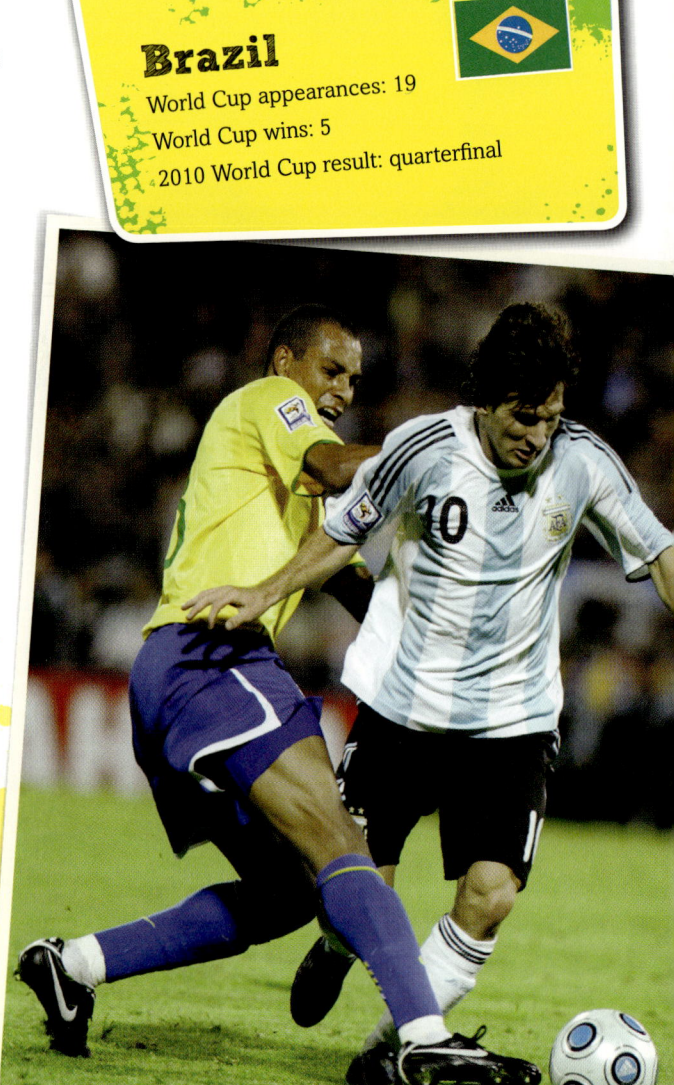

▶ Brazil's Gilberto Silva (left) struggles for the ball with Lionel Messi of Argentina during a 2010 World Cup qualifing match.

FOUR-TIME WINNERS

Italy is always one of the favorites to win the World Cup trophy. They have a very good history at the World Cup, and have won the tournament four times. Italy's last success came at the 2006 World Cup. Italy's team contains experienced players, such as Gianluigi Buffon and Andrea Pirlo, and very skillful attacking players, including Mario Balotelli (see page 24).

TEAM PROFILE
Italy
World Cup appearances: 17
World Cup wins: 4
2010 World Cup result: group stage

TEAM PROFILE
England
World Cup appearances: 13
World Cup wins: 1
2010 World Cup result: second round

▼ England captain Steven Gerrard in action during the 2010 World Cup.

HUGE EXPECTATION

England has qualified for the last four World Cup tournaments, but since 1966 they haven't advanced past the quarterfinal stage. England last played in the World Cup final when they won the tournament in 1966. England has a good mix of experienced players, such as Steven Gerrard, alongside some very talented young players, including Alex Oxlade-Chamberlain (see page 26).

ON THE WAY UP?

Uruguay has not reached the final of the World Cup since 1950, when they won the tournament. In South Africa in 2010, they played extremely well to reach the semifinal. The team will be hoping to go one stage farther this time and reach the final. Uruguay's Diego Forlan was named as the Player of the Tournament for his performances at the 2010 World Cup.

TEAM PROFILE

Uruguay
World Cup appearances: 11
World Cup wins: 2
2010 World Cup result: semifinal

CONSISTENT PERFORMERS

The United States' best result at the World Cup is the quarterfinal in 2002. They have played at the last six tournaments and have a team full of experienced players, such as their star strikers Landon Donovan and Clint Dempsey (see below, right).

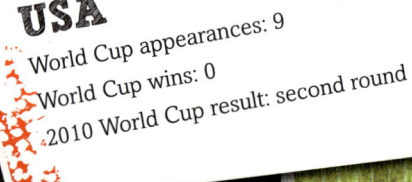

TEAM PROFILE

USA
World Cup appearances: 9
World Cup wins: 0
2010 World Cup result: second round

TEAM PROFILE

Australia

World Cup appearances: 3
World Cup wins: 0
2010 World Cup result: group stage

HOPING FOR A BETTER RESULT

Australia is playing in its third consecutive World Cup. At the 2010 World Cup, the team narrowly missed out on qualifying for the second round on goal difference.

RECENT SUCCESS

Ivory Coast has qualified for the two most recent World Cup competitions and is considered to be one of the best teams from Africa. Many of the Ivory Coast team play in the best leagues in the world, including the English Premier League. Their most famous player is the captain, Didier Drogba.

TEAM PROFILE

Ivory Coast

World Cup appearances: 2
World Cup wins: 0
2010 World Cup result: group stage

REPEAT WINNERS?

Spain won their first ever World Cup in 2010. Spain played very impressively throughout the tournament, and the team is full of outstanding players with amazing skill and passing ability. Spain's midfield includes superstars Xavi Hernandez, Andrés Iniesta, and Cesc Fàbregas (see page 20).

TEAM PROFILE

Spain
World Cup appearances: 13
World Cup wins: 1
2010 World Cup result: winners

TEAM PROFILE

Argentina
World Cup appearances: 15
World Cup wins: 2
2010 World Cup result: quarterfinal

WORLD CUP EXPERIENCE

Argentina won the World Cup the last time it was played on the South American continent in 1978, when they hosted the tournament. The country has a proud tradition in the World Cup, and last competed in the final in 1990 in Italy. Argentina has a team full of brilliant attacking players, many of whom have valuable World Cup experience.

UNFORTUNATE RECORD

The Netherlands were beaten 1–0 by Spain in the final of the 2010 World Cup. It was the third time that the Dutch team had reached the World Cup final. The Netherlands has the unfortunate record of being the only team to have played in three finals and lost all of them. In 2014 they will be hoping to go one stage farther and win in the final. Arjen Robben, Rafael Van Der Vaart, and Wesley Sneijder all played for the Netherlands in the 2010 World Cup, and their experience will be vital for the Netherlands in 2014.

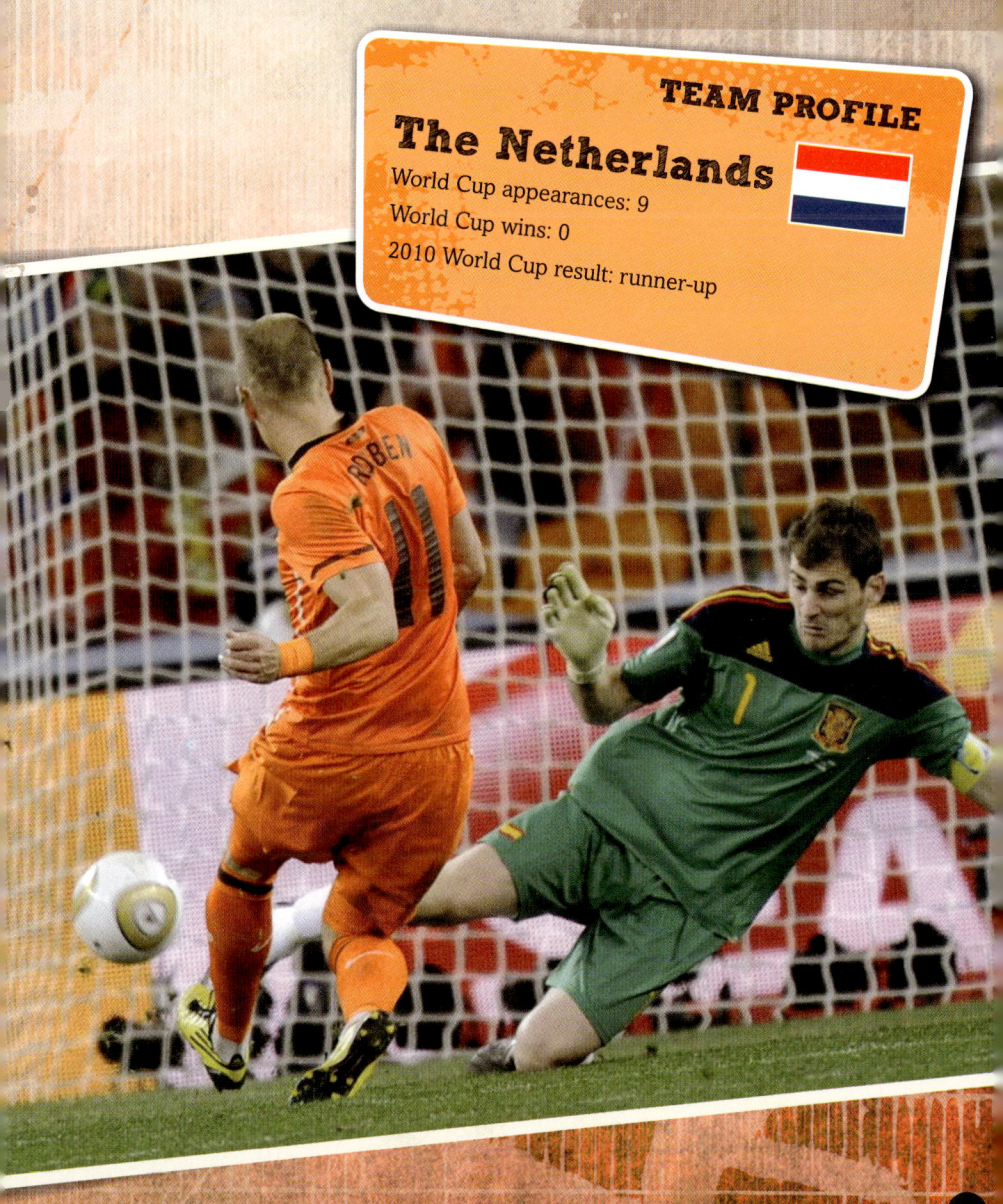

TEAM PROFILE

The Netherlands

World Cup appearances: 9
World Cup wins: 0
2010 World Cup result: runner-up

PLAYERS TO WATCH

Here is a selection of well-known players from around the world who will be showing off their skills at the 2014 World Cup in Brazil.

CRISTIANO RONALDO – PORTUGAL

Cristiano Ronaldo is one of the most famous and recognizable soccer players in the world. At club level he has won league titles in both Spain and England, and he has played in two UEFA Champions League finals. Ronaldo's amazing dribbling ability, technique, and goal-scoring skill mean that he is considered to be one of the greatest players in the world. Ronaldo will be appearing at his third World Cup.

LIONEL MESSI – ARGENTINA

Possibly the greatest soccer player for a generation, Lionel Messi will be appearing in his third World Cup in 2014. This extraordinary and exciting player will be hoping to help Argentina improve on their performance at the past two tournaments. With a combination of agility, pace, dribbling, and precise shooting, Messi has the ability to win any match.

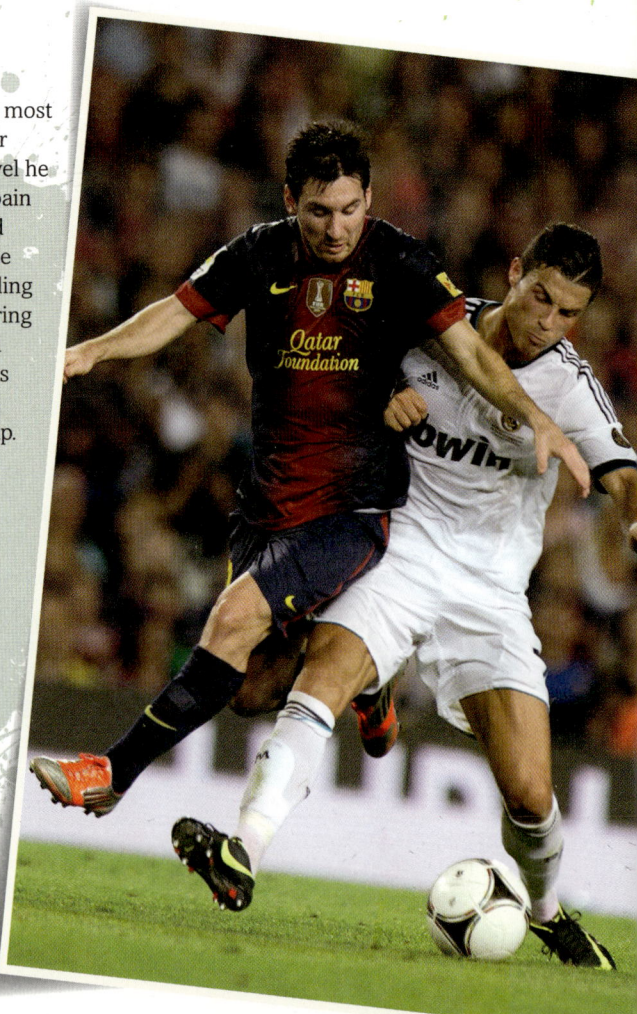

LUIS SUÁREZ – URUGUAY

This controversial striker was one of the stars of the 2010 World Cup. He scored some great goals, but he was also sent off for a handball foul in one match. In 2014 he will be appearing at the World Cup for the second time. Suárez has amazing dribbling skills and a fierce shot.

MESUT ÖZIL – GERMANY

This outstanding midfielder is one of Germany's most important players. His slight build belies his strength and persistence on the field. He is very skillful, has a good passing ability, and is capable of scoring great goals. Özil will be playing in his second World Cup for Germany.

▲ Luis Suárez of Uruguay (far right) is sent off by the referee after handling the ball on the goal line during the 2010 World Cup quarterfinal match against Ghana.

CESC FÀBREGAS – SPAIN

One of the best and most consistent midfielders in the world, Fàbregas joined his hometown club Barcelona from Arsenal in 2011. Fàbregas is a regular performer in the Spanish midfield, which is full of very talented players. Fàbregas has the ability to pass precisely and score important goals. He scored two goals to help Spain win the 2012 UEFA European Championship.

IKER CASILLAS – SPAIN

Spain's World Cup 2010 winning captain is one of the most experienced players at the tournament in 2014. The Spanish goalkeeper is a very well respected player all around the world, and has already played for his country at three World Cups. With over 100 appearances for Spain, Casillas is the most experienced member of their team.

SERGIO AGUERO – ARGENTINA

Sergio Aguero (see above) is a very talented striker who cost Manchester City in the English Premier League over $44 million (£30 million) when he signed for them in 2011. He was instrumental in helping the team to win its first league title since 1968, scoring goals and setting up chances for his teammates. With his amazing talent, Aguero has the ability to take the World Cup by storm and transfer his fantastic form for his team onto the biggest stage.

YAYA TOURE – IVORY COAST

Yaya Toure has become an outstanding player in recent years. He has played for two of the biggest clubs in the world, Barcelona and Manchester City, and has won the league title with both teams. This strong midfielder has all of the attributes that a great modern player should have, including pace, strength, technique, and determination.

SHINJI KAGAWA – JAPAN

Since moving from Japan to Europe in 2010, Shinji Kagawa has continued to improve and is now considered to be a world class player. Kagawa will be Japan's most recognizable player at the 2014 World Cup. He is fast, skillful, and can score impressive goals.

DID YOU KNOW?

When Shinji Kagawa joined Manchester United in 2012 he became the first Japanese player to play for the prestigious English club.

JAVIER HERNANDEZ – MEXICO

Another talented young Manchester United player, this Mexican striker drew a lot of attention with his performances for his country at the 2010 World Cup. Soon after the tournament, Hernandez was snapped up by United. Hernandez is a very composed goalscorer and takes his opportunities well.

▲ Shinji Kagawa celebrates a goal during a match in the English Premier League.

GIANLUIGI BUFFON – ITALY

Gianluigi Buffon (see above, left) has played in goal for Italy over 120 times, and has appeared for his country at three World Cup competitions. Buffon's impressive performances in goal in 2006 helped Italy reach the final and win the World Cup for the first time since 1982.

JOE HART – ENGLAND

Unfortunate not to have the chance to play at the 2010 World Cup in South Africa, Joe Hart (see above, right) has since firmly established himself as England's first-choice goalkeeper. Hart has a lot of experience for a young goalkeeper, and is improving all the time. He is now considered to be one of the best goalkeepers in the world.

WORLD CUP FIRST TIMERS

Here are some new World Cup players for you to watch out for.

These young stars will be playing in the World Cup for the first time, and will have to cope with the pressure of performing on the biggest stage in soccer.

MARIO BALOTELLI – ITALY

Italy striker Mario Balotelli (see below) is a controversial figure who has the potential to win any match he is playing in. He has incredible strength and shooting ability. Balotelli scored three goals to help his team reach the final of the UEFA European Championship in 2012.

EDEN HAZARD – BELGIUM

Eden Hazard is the most exciting and skillful player to come from Belgium since the 1980s. In 2012, English club Chelsea reportedly paid an extraordinary $51 million to sign this talented midfielder. Hazard has the potential to score goals or set them up for his teammates.

▼ Colombia striker Falcao celebrates after scoring a goal.

FALCAO – COLOMBIA

Since moving from South America to play club soccer in Europe, Falcao just has not stopped scoring! He has won the UEFA Europa League twice, in 2011 and 2012, and finished top goalscorer in the competition in 2012. He also scored a tremendous hat-trick against Chelsea in the 2012 UEFA European Super Cup when Spanish club Athletico Madrid won 4–1.

JORDAN AYEW – GHANA

Ghanaian striker Jordan Ayew is an exciting young talent who is improving all the time. This attacking player has a lot of natural ability, and can score goals. If he can keep his concentration and composure in front of goal, he could have a great World Cup.

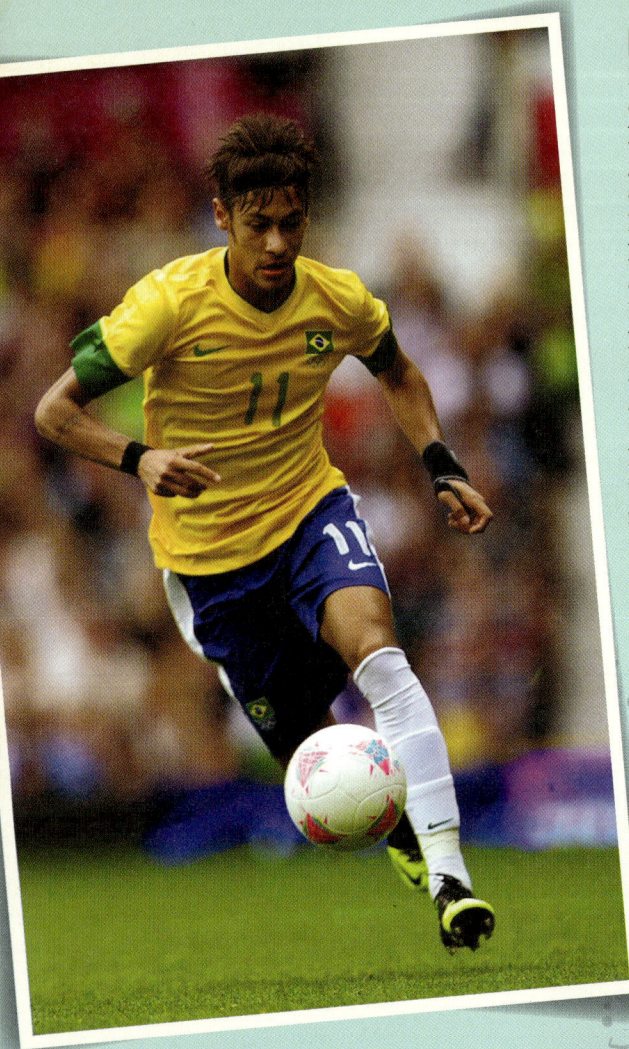

NEYMAR – BRAZIL

Neymar (see left) is an outstanding talent who has already scored many great goals for Brazil in his career. Neymar is the latest Brazilian striker in a long line of amazing, skillful, attacking players. Pelé, Romario, and Ronaldo have all been important goalscorers when Brazil has gone on to win the World Cup. Neymar will hope that his goals can fire Brazil into the World Cup final for the first time since 2002.

ALEX OXLADE-CHAMBERLAIN – ENGLAND

This athletic, fast, and skillful player was signed by English Premiership club Arsenal for $19 million when he was only 17 years old. This is a massive amount of money to pay for such a young player. Oxlade-Chamberlain appears to have all the skills and ability necessary to make his mark on the World Cup.

DID YOU KNOW?

Because of his name and impressive physique, Alex Oxlade-Chamberlain is nicknamed "the Ox."

SOULEYMANE COULIBALY – IVORY COAST

Watch out for this young striker at the 2014 World Cup. He is a fast-improving player, and could play an important role for the Ivory Coast team at the tournament.

MARIO GÖTZE – GERMANY

Götze (see below) is considered to be one of the most talented young players ever to play for Germany. Götze made his Germany debut at the age of 18. This exciting young midfielder is full of tricks and can pass the ball very accurately.

DID YOU KNOW?

Götze became Germany's joint-youngest goalscorer in history when he scored against Brazil in August 2011 aged just 19 years and 68 days.

MANAGER PROFILES

LUIZ FELIPE SCOLARI – BRAZIL

Scolari was appointed as the manager of Brazil in November 2012. He replaced Mano Menezes, who had failed in his bid to guide Brazil to a gold medal in the 2012 Olympic soccer tournament. Scolari is a well-respected coach, and has had a successful career as a club manager in Brazil and as the national team manager. His previous spell in charge of his country ended with sucess at the 2002 World Cup. There is a huge amount of pressure on Scolari and his team to repeat that triumph on home soil in 2014.

VICENTE DEL BOSQUE – SPAIN

Spain's manager Vicente Del Bosque (see below) will be attempting to accomplish a feat at the World Cup that has not been achieved since 1962. Spain will try to retain the title of World Champions, just as Brazil did following their success at the 1958 tournament. Del Bosque is a very experienced manager and has guided Spain to recent success at the 2012 UEFA European Championships. His team is full of outstandingly talented players, and they have a great chance of winning their second World Cup trophy in 2014.

▼ Jurgen Klinsman (far left) jumps high above the opposition players to head the ball during the 1990 World Cup.

JURGEN KLINSMANN - USA

Ex-Germany international Jurgen Klinsmann was appointed manager of the United States team in 2011. It is his second assignment as an international manager. Klinsmann led his own country to the semifinal of the 2006 World Cup in Germany.

DID YOU KNOW?

Jurgen Klinsmann used to be a striker and was part of the West Germany team that won the World Cup in 1990 in Italy. Klinsmann scored three goals in 1990 to help his team reach the final.

29

FABIO CAPELLO – RUSSIA

Fabio Capello is one of the most successful club managers in history. He has won league titles with four different teams, including Juventus and Real Madrid. Capello was appointed England manager in 2007 and was manager of the team at the 2010 World Cup. England didn't play very well, and was beaten 4–1 by Germany in the second round. Capello resigned from the post of England manager in 2012. Russia wanted an experienced man to help them qualify for the 2014 World Cup, and Capello was an obvious choice. Capello's contract with Russia makes him one of the highest-paid managers in the world.

▼ Fabio Capello found his time as England manager very frustrating.

ROY HODGSON – ENGLAND

Roy Hodgson was appointed England manager after Fabio Capello resigned from the job in 2012. He started his England career with a solid record of only one defeat in his first five matches in charge. Hodgson is a very experienced manager and has previously managed three other nations, including Finland and the United Arab Emirates. Hodgson guided Switzerland to the 1994 World Cup, and has also managed prestigious European clubs such as Internazionale and Liverpool.

JOACHIM LÖW – GERMANY

Joachim Löw (see above) is gaining more experience as a manager all the time. He took over as manager of Germany after the 2006 World Cup, during which he worked as an assistant to the manager. Löw has brought together a group of players who are young and exciting to watch. His team plays fast, attractive, attacking soccer. Löw was in charge of Germany at the 2010 World Cup and the team reached the semifinal.

CITIES AND STADIUMS

Twelve cities in Brazil will host matches at the 2014 World Cup, each with something different to offer.

Here you can find information about the vibrant cities as well as the stadiums where the matches will be played.

CURITIBA

Stadium: Estadio Joaquim Américo

Built: 1914

Capacity: 40,000

Curitiba is on the south coast of Brazil. The city name of Curitiba means "pine nut." It is called this because of all the pine trees that grow in the area. The Estadio Joaquim Américo, also known as Arena da Baixada, has been completely refurbished for the World Cup. The home stadium of Brazilian league club Atlético Paranaesne, it will host four World Cup matches.

◀ **This map shows the cities where games will be played in 2014.**

▲ This is a computer-generated model of the Estadio das Dunas.

NATAL
Stadium: Estadio das Dunas

Built: 2013

Capacity: 42,086

Natal has many sandy beaches and sand dunes, and it is a very popular destination for tourists. The "Stadium of the Dunes" is named after the impressive sand dunes in Natal.

CUIABÁ
Stadium: Arena Pantanal

Built: 2014

Capacity: 42,968

Cuiabá is known as the "green city." The city is very popular with tourists who come to see the incredible variety of nature and visit the different areas that include savannah, wetlands, and the Amazon River. The new stadium was built for the 2014 World Cup and will host four matches during the tournament.

DID YOU KNOW?

Cuiabá is located exactly in the center of South America. It is 1,242 miles (2,000 kilometers) from both the Pacific and Atlantic Oceans.

BELO HORIZONTE

Stadium: Estadio Mineirao

Built: 1965

Capacity: 66,805

Located southeast of the capital Brasilia, Belo Horizonte is the sixth largest city in Brazil with a population of 2.4 million people. The stadium has been modernized to be used as a venue for the World Cup, and will host one of the semifinal matches. Estadio Mineirao is the home stadium of two former Brazilian league champions, Atlético Mineirao and Cruzeiro. These two teams are local rivals.

DID YOU KNOW?

Former Brazil soccer star and World Cup winner Ronaldo started his career with Cruzeiro.

FORTALEZA

Stadium: Estadio Castelao

Built: 1973

Capacity: 64,165

The vibrant city of Fortaleza is a popular destination for tourists, with sandy beaches, plenty of sunshine, and a party atmosphere. The two historic clubs of Ceará Sporting Club and Fortaleza Esporte Club come from Fortaleza. It boasts one of the biggest soccer stadiums in Brazil, the Estadio Castelao, which has been modernized to be a venue for the 2013 Confederations Cup and the World Cup in 2014. The stadium has a new roof and the locker rooms have been upgraded.

MANAUS

Stadium: Arena Amazonia

Built: 2013

Capacity: 42,377

Manaus is the largest city in the Amazon rain forest region of Brazil, known as Amazonia. It has a warm and tropical climate all year round, and in the summer temperatures can reach up to 104 degrees Fahrenheit (40 degrees Celsius). The players at the World Cup could well suffer in the heat. Four matches will be played at this stadium during the 2014 World Cup. The stadium has been rebuilt recently, and is surrounded by a metal structure that looks like a straw basket. The Amazonia region is well known for producing these types of baskets.

▼ The Estadio Castelao in Fortaleza, Brazil.

RIO DE JANEIRO

Stadium: Estadio do Maracana

Built: 1950

Capacity: 76,935

Rio de Janeiro is the second largest city in Brazil, with a population of over six million people. It is a beautiful city and was the capital of Brazil until 1960. Rio is home to four of Brazil's most well supported football clubs, including Flamengo, the most popular club in Brazil.

One of the most famous football stadiums in the world, the Maracana stadium, was built as a venue for the 1950 World Cup. It is being completely rebuilt for the 2014 World Cup, and it will host seven matches, including the final.

▲ The Estadio do Maracana before a friendly match between Brazil and England in 2013.

DID YOU KNOW?

People born and raised in Rio de Janeiro are known as "Cariocas."

BRASILIA

Stadium: Estadio Nacional

Built: 2012

Capacity: 70,042

Brasilia, the capital of Brazil, is close to the center of the country. Many important government buildings are located here. The Estadio National was built in place of a former stadium that was named in honor of the Brazil World Cup legend, Garrincha. This venue will host seven World Cup matches, including one quarterfinal. The opening match of the 2013 Confederations Cup was played at this stadium.

PORTO ALEGRE

Stadium: Estadio Beira Rio

Built: 1969

Capacity: 50,287

Porto Alegre is the most southern city to host matches at the 2014 World Cup. It is home to two of Brazil's most famous and successful soccer clubs, Gremio and Internacional. Both of these teams have won the Copa Libertadores on two occasions. The Estadio Beira Rio stadium has been upgraded, including the addition of a new roof, and will be the venue for five matches at the World Cup.

▼ The Japan team warm up under the stadium lights at Estadio Nacional in 2013.

SALVADOR

Stadium: Arena Fonte Nova

Built: 2012

Capacity: 56,000

Salvador is an attractive city on the east coast. It is the state capital of the Bahia region and the third biggest city in Brazil. This new stadium was constructed on the site of a previous stadium that was demolished in 2010. The new stadium includes shops, restaurants, and a museum of soccer. It will host six matches in 2014.

SÃO PAULO

Stadium: Arena de São Paulo

Built: 2014

Capacity: 65,807

São Paulo is the largest city in Brazil, with a population of over 11 million people. São Paulo has a very mixed population, with people from more than 100 different ethnic backgrounds living together here. Three major soccer teams are based in the city: Palmeiras, Corinthians, and São Paulo. The newly built Arena de São Paulo will be the venue for the opening match of the 2014 World Cup. It will host six matches during the tournament, including one of the semifinals.

RECIFE

Stadium: Arena Pernambuco

Built: 2013

Capacity: 43,921

The city of Recife is located on the northeast coast of Brazil. It is named after the Portuguese word for "reef." Recife is well known for its soccer-loving population. Named in honor of the Brazilian state of Pernambuco, this is a brand new stadium that was built for the 2014 World Cup. The stadium is part of a larger complex that includes shops and restaurants.

DID YOU KNOW?

The residents of São Paulo are known as "Paulistanos."

▼ The city of São Paulo will host six matches at the 2014 World Cup, including the opening match of the tournament.

WORLD CUP 2014: THE TEAMS

NATION	PREVIOUS WORLD CUP APPEARANCES	BEST FINISH IN A WORLD CUP	STAR PLAYER
Algeria	2	Group stage 1982, 1986, 2010	Soufiane Feghouli
Argentina	15	Winners 1978, 1986	Lionel Messi
Australia	3	Second round 2006	Tim Cahill
Belgium	11	Fourth 1996	Eden Hazard
Bosnia-Herzegovina	0	–	Edin Džeko
Brazil	19	Winners 1958, 1962, 1970, 1994, 2002	Neymar
Cameroon	6	Quarter-final 1990	Samuel Eto'o
Colombia	4	Second round 1990	Rademal Falcao
Chile	8	Third 1962	Alexis Sánchez
Costa Rica	3	Second round 1990	Bryan Ruiz
Croatia	3	Third 1998	Mario Mandžukic
England	13	Winners 1966	Steven Gerrard
Ecuador	2	Second round 2006	Antonio Valencia
France	13	Winners 1998	Franck Ribéry
Germany	17	Winners 1954, 1974, 1990	Mesut Özil
Ghana	2	Quarter final 2010	Asamoah Gyan

NATION	PREVIOUS WORLD CUP APPEARANCES	BEST FINISH IN A WORLD CUP	STAR PLAYER
Greece	2	Group stage 1994, 2010	Kostas Mitroglou
Honduras	2	Group stage 1982, 2010	Emilio Izaguirre
Iran	3	Group stage 1978, 1998, 2006	Ashkan Dejagah
Italy	17	Winners 1934, 1938, 1982, 2006	Mario Balotelli
Ivory Coast	2	Group stage 2006, 2010	Didier Drogba
Japan	4	Second round 2002, 2010	Keisuke Honda
Mexico	14	Quarter-final 1970, 1986	Javier Hernández
Netherlands	9	Runners-up 1974, 1978,	Robin van Persie
Nigeria	4	Second round 1994, 1998	Victor Moses
Portugal	5	Third 1966	Cristiano Ronaldo
Russia	9	Fourth 1966	Roman Shirokov
South Korea	8	Fourth 2002	Son Heung-Min
Spain	13	Winners 2010	Andres Iniesta
Switzerland	9	Quarter-final 1934, 1938, 1954	Xherdan Shaqiri
Uruguay	11	Winners 1930, 1950	Luis Suárez
USA	9	Third 1930	Clint Dempsey

WORLD CUP 2014: MATCH SCHEDULE

GROUP MATCHES

Venue	Thu Jun 12	Fri Jun 13	Sat Jun 14	Sun Jun 15	Mon Jun 16	Tue Jun 17	Wed Jun 18	Thu Jun 19	Fri Jun 20	Sat Jun 21	Sun Jun 22	Mon Jun 23	Tue Jun 24	Wed Jun 25	Thu Jun 26
Belo Horizonte Estadio Mineirao			5 C1vC2			15 H1vH2				27 F1vF3			40 D2vD3		
Brasilia Estadio Nacional				9 E1vE2				21 C1vC3				33 A4vA1			46 G2vG3
Cuiaba Arena Pantanal		4 B3vB4				16 H3vH4				28 F4vF2			37 C4vC1		
Curitiba Arena da Baixada					12 F3vF4				26 E4vE2			35 B4vB1			48 H2vH3
Fortaleza Estadio Castelao			7 D1vD2			17 A1vA3				29 G1vG3			38 C2vC3		
Manaus Arena Amazonia			8 D3vD4			18 A4vA2					30 G4vG2			41 E4vE1	
Natal Estadio das Dunas		2 A3vA4			14 G3vG4			22 C4vC2					39 D4vD1		
Porto Alegre Estadio Beira-Rio				10 E3vE4				20 B4vB2				32 H4vH2		43 F4vF1	
Recife Arena Pernambuco			6 C3vC4					24 D4vD2				34 A2vA3			45 G4vG1
Rio de Janeiro Estadio do Maracana				11 F1vF2			19 B1vB3					31 H1vH3		42 E2vE3	
Salvador Arena Fonte Nova		3 B1vB2			13 G1vG2				25 E1vE3				44 F2vF3		
Sao Paulo Arena de Sao Paulo	1 A1vA2							23 D1vD3				36 B2vB3			47 H4vH1

KEY
Teams playing. Team 1 and Team 2 from Group A are playing this game. → 1 A1vA2
— Game number. This is the first game.
— Letters and colour of the circle show the group. For example, Red A = Group A.

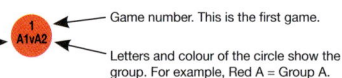

42

Groups

GROUP A		GROUP B		GROUP C		GROUP D	
1. Brazil	3. Mexico	1. Spain	3. Chile	1. Colombia	3. Ivory Coast	1. Uruguay	3. England
2. Croatia	4. Cameroon	2. Netherlands	4. Australia	2. Greece	4. Japan	2. Costa Rica	4. Italy

GROUP E		GROUP F		GROUP G		GROUP H	
1. Switzerland	3. France	1. Argentina	3. Iran	1. Germany	3. Ghana	1. Belgium	3. Russia
2. Ecuador	4. Honduras	2. Bosnia-Herzegovina	4. Nigeria	2. Portugal	4. USA	2. Algeria	4. South Korea

ROUND OF 16

- **49** 1Av2B — Saturday June 28
- **50** 1Cv2D — Saturday June 28
- **51** 1Bv2A — Sunday June 29
- **52** 1Dv2C — Sunday June 29
- **53** 1Ev2F — Monday June 30
- **54** 1Gv2H — Monday June 30
- **55** 1Fv2E — Tuesday July 1
- **56** 1Hv2G — Tuesday July 1

QUARTER-FINALS

- **57** W49 v W50 — Friday July 4
- **58** W53 v W54 — Friday July 4
- **59** W51 v W52 — Saturday July 5
- **60** W55 v W56 — Saturday July 5

SEMI-FINALS

- **61** W57 v W58 — Tuesday July 8
- **62** W59 v W60 — Wednesday July 9

3/4 PLACE AND FINAL

- **63** Loser I v Loser II — Saturday July 12
- **64** Winner I v Winner II — Sunday July 13

Rest Days: Wednesday July 2 – Thursday July 3; Sunday July 6 – Monday July 7; Thursday July 10 – Friday July 11.

After the group matches, the top two teams from each group go through to the last 16. So, each group has a 1, 2, team. For example, Group D = 1D and 2D. 1D is the team who came top of Group D. 2D is the team who came second.

GLOSSARY

architect someone whose job is to design buildings

colonize form a colony on. A colony is a place that is under the control of another country.

Confederations Cup FIFA tournament that is held every four years and is contested by the winners of the previous World Cup and the six FIFA confederation championships

continent one of the world's largest land masses. Continents are usually divided into many countries. There are seven continents on Earth.

Copa Libertadores prestigious soccer tournament held in South America for South American club teams

debut someone making their first appearance. For example, soccer players at the World Cup for the first time are making their debut.

democratically voted for by the population

demolish knock down, or destroy

extra time extra period of play that is added to a soccer match if it is a draw at the end of regulation time (90 minutes). Extra time lasts for 30 minutes, with two halves of 15 minutes each.

Fédération Internationale de Football Association (FIFA) International organization responsible for soccer around the world

goal difference difference between the goals scored and conceded by a team. If a team has scored 1 goal and conceded 2, then the team has a goal difference of -1.

Grand Prix international motor race

handball foul committed during a match when a player touches the ball with their hand

independence freedom from outside control

inaugural marking or celebrating the beginning of something

league group of teams that play matches against each other

legend (of a person) extremely famous person who is well known for their particular talent or success

military dictatorship form of government where all power rests with the armed forces

Olympics international sport competition held every four years

prestigious something that is very important or special

refurbish clean and restore something to its original condition

republic state in which power is held by the people through elected representatives

rival person with whom one competes

savannah grassy plain with few trees

UEFA Europa League soccer tournament that is held in Europe for European club teams

UEFA European Championship tournament that takes place every four years between European national teams

vibrant bright, or full of energy

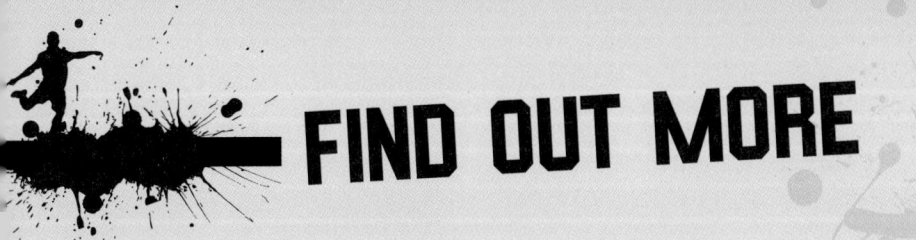

FIND OUT MORE

BOOKS
Buckley, Jr., James. *Pelé*. New York: Dorling Kindersley, 2007.

Gifford, Clive. *Kingfisher Soccer Encyclopedia*. New York: Macmillan, 2010.

Hornby, Hugh. *Eyewitness: Soccer*. Dorling Kindersley, 2010.

Hurley, Michael. *World Cup Fever: A – Z of the World Cup*. Chicago: Raintree, 2014.

Hurley, Michael. *World Cup Fever: World Cup Heroes*. Chicago: Raintree, 2014.

Hurley, Michael. *World Cup Fever: World Cup Nations*. Chicago: Raintree, 2014.

WEBSITES
www.fifa.com
The official website for everything World Cup related. You can find the latest team and player news, games, results, and photos.

www.fifa.com/worldcup/destination/index.html
This is a great place to find out more information about the country of Brazil. There is information about the cities that will host matches during the World Cup and the stadiums where the matches will be played.

en.mascot.fifa.com
Follow Fuleco, the official mascot for the World Cup in Brazil. Catch up on the latest news, play games, and check out photos of Fuleco.

www.ussoccer.com
The official website of the U.S. Soccer Federation provides news and coverage of all U.S. players and teams.

www.fifa.com/classicfootball/index.html?intcmp=fifacom_hp_ module_classic_football
Check out match reports on important World Cup matches from the past, and find out more about some of the greatest ever players, teams, and stadiums around the world.

www.footballworldcupbrazil2014.com/
This unofficial guide to the 2014 World Cup provides videos, blogs, team profiles, and facts and figures about previous World Cup tournaments.

kids.nationalgeographic.com/kids/places/find/brazil/
If you want to know more about Brazil and the history, geography, and culture of the country, this is a great place to start.

LOOK IT UP...

1. Brazil is hosting the World Cup for the second time. Do you know or can you find out which other countries have hosted the tournament more than once?

2. Do you know or can you find out which famous soccer stadium was used for the final of the World Cup when it was played in Brazil in 1950?

3. The second-longest river in the world runs through Brazil. Do you know the name of this famous river?

4. Brazil is such a large country that it has a border with every country in South America except two. Do you know or can you find out which South American countries do not share a border with Brazil?

INDEX

2010 World Cup 5, 13, 14, 15, 16, 17, 19, 20, 22, 30, 31

Aguero, Sergio 20
Argentina 4, 12, 16, 18, 20
Australia 15
Ayew, Jordan 25

Balotelli, Mario 13, 24
Belgium 25
Belo Horizonte 34
Brasilia 11, 37
Brazil 4, 6, 8–11, 12, 26, 27, 28, 32–33
Buffon, Gianluigi 13, 23
Bündchen, Gisele 11

Capello, Fabio 30
Casillars, Iker 20
Colombia 25
Coulibaly, Souleymane 27
Cuiabá 33
Curitiba 32

Del Bosque, Vincent 28
Dempsey, Clint 14
Donovan, Landon 14

England 4, 13, 23, 26, 30, 31

Fàbregas, Cesc 16, 20
Falcao 25
final 6, 36
first World Cup 4
Forlan, Diego 14
Fortaleza 34
France 4
Fuleco 6

Germany/West Germany 4, 19, 27, 29, 30, 31

Gerrard, Steven 13
Ghana 19, 25
goalkeepers 20, 23
Götze, Mario 27
gold stars 4
group matches 6

Hart, Joe 23
Hazard, Eden 25
Hernandez, Javier 22
Hernandez, Xavi 16
Hodgson, Roy 31
host cities 32–39

Iniesta, Andrés 16
Italy 4, 13, 23, 24
Ivory Coast 15, 21, 27

Japan 22

Kagawa, Shinji 22
Klinsmann, Jurgen 29
knockout competition 6

Löw, Joachim 31

managers 28–31
Manaus 34
Maracana Stadium 36
Mascherano, Javier 16
mascot 6
Massa, Felipe 11
Messi, Lionel 12, 18
Mexico 22

Natal 33
The Netherlands 5, 17
Neymar 26
Niemeyer, Oscar 11

Olympic Games 4, 8
Oxlade-Chamberlain, Alex 13, 26
Özil, Mesut 19

Pelé 10, 26
Pirlo, Andrea 13
players to watch 18–27
Porto Alegre 37
Portugal 18

qualifying matches 6

Recife 38
Rio de Janeiro 6, 8, 36
Robben, Arjen 17
Romario 26
Ronaldinho 10
Ronaldo 26, 34
Ronaldo, Cristiano 18
Russia 30

Salvador 38
São Paulo 6, 8, 38, 39
schedule 6, 42–43
Scolari, Luiz Felipe 28
Sneijder, Wesley 17
Spain 4, 5, 16, 17, 20, 28
stadiums 32–39
Suarez, Luis 19
Switzerland 31

teams to watch 12–17
Toure, Yaya 21

UEFA Champions League 18
UEFA Europa League 25
UEFA European Championship 20, 24, 28
UEFA European Super Cup 25
United States 14, 29
Uruguay 4, 14, 19

Van Der Vaart, Rafael 17